Rea

SUNDROPS ON LIFE:
A BOOK OF GOOD THOUGHTS

"Sundrops on Life contains truth the soul craves and quite a few of the quotes may affect you on the emotional level ... Time after time, these quotes surprised and enlightened me in a deeper wisdom that the heart knows..."Sundrops On Life" is a book that brings you back to the present while you contemplate how you will live in the future. Truly healing!"

Rebecca Johnson, The RebeccaReview.com

"To have an entire book of fresh, new perspectives is just amazing! Each and every one is just rich and a true nugget of a jewel... This is such an original, lovely book, I promise you will be as charmed as I have been"

Kathy Dannel Vitcak, Editor, The Bookworm

"Spanning themes of worry, hope, health, strength, relationships, faith, anger, children and more, Sundrops on Life is replete with sagacious wisdom and unusual perspectives... If your soul craves wisdom, it will find nourishment through Patrick's luminous Sundrops."

Janet Boyer, Top 500 Amazon Reviewer

"Sundrops serve as consistent inspiration allowing us to quiet the mind, even for just a moment, and experience the value of moving in a positive direction."

Dan Tobin, M.D, Author (*Peaceful Dying, Shelter from the Storm*), Professor, and CEO

"I am grateful that Patrick McBride's wisdom is available in this book. Don't miss an opportunity to read it, then buy a copy for a friend."

Reader review on Amazon

"Patrick McBride's Sundrops are truly unique and special. Patrick receives bits of wisdom that are remarkable for their insight and, especially, their compassion. His Sundrops are never trite or cliché, but instead cut right to the heart of the human condition with love and understanding that is rare these days."

MM, San Francisco, CA, Reader review on Amazon

"I had a note today from a really good friend who told me her daughter had had a terrible car crash in February and is now on the mend. She told me that that Sundrops have been a wonderful help to her during this time. See the pebble in the still water how it ripples out to all those that you don't see."

BG, TX

"I'm having to make some major decisions regarding my professional life and your Sundrops are speaking so much life into my situation. I'm also more cognizant of my attitude towards life and those I come in contact with on a daily basis. I thank Heaven for giving you those special "Sundrops" to share with us!"

VW, Fort Worth, T X

SUNDROPS

ON LIFE A BOOK OF GOOD THOUGHTS

PATRICK McBRIDE
WWW.PATRICKINSPIRES.COM

SUNDROPS ON LIFE:
A BOOK OF GOOD THOUGHTS

Copyright © 2003-2009 by Patrick McBride

Address inquiries to:

Allistar Publishing
3000 Custer Rd #270-331
Plano, TX 75075
or to:

patrick@patrickinspires.com

ISBN 978-0-615-32674-0

Produced in the United States of America
Second Printing, November 2009

DEDICATION

This book and my life are dedicated to my
Angel Jane, the light on my path and in my heart,
and to my greatest blessings: Jessica, Kristen,
Heather, Brandon and Michael.

ACKNOWLEDGMENTS

This book would still be just a thought and a large pile of scraps of paper if it were not for the love and dedication of a dear friend, Elaine Brzezinski. She took the initiative and the time to copy every single Sundrop (there are thousands) on separate pages so that they could be sorted into categories, a huge task. Thanks to Lauren Winter and Lynda Mane for the hours and hours of typing and revisions. Thanks to all of the people whom I will never meet who made it possible for you to be holding this book right now.

PREFACE

I once heard that Sundrops were just like Hershey's Kisses. At first glance, they are beautiful but if you actually pick one up and take the time to unwrap it, it is even more enjoyable.

I've always loved quotes. Several years ago, I wrote a simple uplifting newsletter that went out to a small number of people. On the last page each week would be a handful of quotes from well known persons. The quotes would cause one to think, to ponder, maybe even to change one's way of looking at something.

One day, several years ago, I was short a few quotes and too lazy to look one up when two profound thoughts came to me. I wrote them down, attributing them to no one and thought no more of it. Up until that issue, there had been no feedback on the quotes that I printed each week, but all of a sudden everyone wanted to know the author or the works of the last two quotes. I ignored them all, happy to have created a little mystery for once in my life. The following week I added more, and soon the whole back page was filled with these anonymous quotes that just seemed to come forth when I intended them.

As the months passed, the weekly newsletter disappeared and the quotes now known as Sundrops became a daily posting. Each morning I sit down, quiet myself, say a short prayer and clear my thoughts of the mundane, so that somehow, words that will positively affect even one person in need will come through. Sometimes, an inner voice will admonish me to erase what I have written and write another because what I had written was not a Sundrop.

The feedback each morning from the lives that are touched by these words has fed my heart and soul for a number of years now. I am both grateful and honored. The same clarity that I seek for Sundrops to appear has helped me in all areas of my life. Even the title of this book came through this way. I believe that if we can learn to quiet ourselves, great things will then pour forth from all of us. I love and enjoy Sundrops, but I write them for you.

Unwrap and enjoy.

Love and Blessings,
Patrick

CONTENTS

1. Perspective & Wisdom 1

2. Worry..25

3. Hope 41

4. Happiness..47

5. The Present 59

6. Love 67

7. Health 83

8. Strength..89

9. Anger...95

10. Relationships 103

11. Children 115

12. Faith 119

PERSPECTIVE & WISDOM

Peace of mind comes from the realization that the
worries we believe to be so important right
now are no different from the worries of the past
that now seem so senseless.

Sometimes we are out of balance because of what's
going on around us and sometimes we just think we
are out of balance because we are growing.

CHAPTER ONE

One of the reasons that animals are so endearing to most of us is because we don't get defensive if they can do something better than us.

If there is something in your life that is not to your liking, work on changing it. If it can't be changed, work on changing how you perceive it.

'Tis nothing so bold as to look at all without judgment. 'Tis nothing in life that is rewarded more beautifully.

The road from here on is filled with obstacles. What is not readily recalled is that the road to here was filled with obstacles. That's life.

CHAPTER ONE

The real thrill in life is not in waiting to live
a life that is close to perfect but in seeing
the life you live as close to perfect.

We put our problems under a magnifying
glass to study them and that's good.
The anxiety comes from thinking that
they really are that big.

The person who drives straight ahead
when the road turns is never
praised for having a determined will.

The mirror will tell you how you look on
the outside, but it is the eyes of a friend that
will tell you how you look on the inside.

CHAPTER ONE

If we could come to the realization that every
life contains suffering, we could just deal
effectively with the suffering and not waste energy
on the outrage that it happened to us.

Serenity is the ability to make
molehills out of mountains.

It is wisdom that lets us know that we are seeing
everything only from our perspective. It is love that
allows us to accept that in others.

Those people we like, we will always find
a way to excuse them. Those people we do not like,
we will always find a way to accuse them.

CHAPTER ONE

If you couldn't hear the music, the gyrations of
people on the dance floor would seem chaotic.
If you look at the world and see only chaos, maybe
it's because you can't hear the music.

Serenity is the ability to see the sunrise as the
gift wrapping on a precious new day instead of seeing
it as the flash from a starter's gun.

We can easily change the outlook on any moment
by merely asking what's right instead of always asking
what's wrong.

How come we find it so easy to praise and
applaud a sports team of strangers and so hard to praise
and applaud a good person that we know?

CHAPTER ONE

The person who carefully watches the placement
of every footstep will never fall but they will also
never get to see the rainbow overhead.

If you are living your life just
for the weekends, five-sevenths
of your life is being wasted.

If we could focus on the way we love
as much as we focus on the way we look,
we wouldn't mind so much how we look.

The possessions that we now take for granted
were at one time the magic key to contentment;
or so we thought.

CHAPTER ONE

In twenty years you will look back at this
time and think about the endless opportunities
associated with being this age.

We can look at all the colors of nature and see
glory and yet we can look at all the colors of people
and see just the color.

It never, ever helps to be told that
there are people worse off than you when you
are feeling down.

If you could stand aside and watch
yourself think and act for just one day, the
laughter would stay with you for years.

CHAPTER ONE

Why do we have to wait until we only have
a few days left to finally understand that
each day is precious?

The flowers and the color we hunger for
in winter are soon taken for granted in the
warmth of summer.

Tolerance is the ability to realize that beliefs are
many and diverse but all are held as the obvious
truth by the holder.

The first step to being strong and centered is
realizing that something wrong does not
mean everything wrong.

CHAPTER ONE

It's not that we are lacking in great strength.
It's just that the only time we tend to evaluate our
strengths is when we are feeling negative and weak.

You have to play the cards that you have been
dealt but nobody ever said that you couldn't
make some of them wild.

You are not elevated because you put someone
down. You are not right because you made
someone else wrong.

We never behold a stormy day or two and label
all days as stormy and yet we have a bad day
or two and instantly label all of our life as bad.

CHAPTER ONE

Benevolent or malevolent is a judgment
only from our perspective. The same wave that
frightens a fisherman thrills a surfer.

If you really think that we are all the same,
just look into someone else's shopping cart.

Missing meals feels weakening.
Fasting feels energetic. Everything in life is
subject to the category in which you place it.

Is your spiritual life part of your freedom
or part of your bondage?

CHAPTER ONE

The most important moment of growth is
when you decide for that moment to listen and
learn instead of sharing your opinion.

As we grow older, it becomes more and more
obvious that what we take seriously is not all that
serious. What we call obvious, younger
people call wisdom.

To take delight in another person's good fortune
is to prepare the way for your own.

The easiest way to find what dominates your life
is to pay attention to what makes you raise
the volume of your voice. Is it love, laughter,
complaining, song, praise, or anger?

CHAPTER ONE

No one knows exactly when the final note of
their dance is to be played but it is better to
hear it on the dance floor instead of when you
are hurrying to the dance floor.

One of the biggest misconceptions in this life is
to think that other people spend as much time as
we do thinking about our faults and mistakes.

The great test of balance and love is how you react
when someone tells you that you are wrong when
you think you are right.

Welcome the rain like a parched farmer. Welcome all
people like you've been lost alone for a month.
Welcome each day like you've been given an extra one.

CHAPTER ONE

Like a mirage, life without suffering seems to be just ahead but it is just an illusion. Suffering will always be a part of life. The key is not to suffer just for practice.

At some point in your life, it may be very difficult to follow directions. That's when you know that it's not time to follow. It's time to lead.

If you're not enjoying the ride, grabbing the brass ring won't change a thing.

How a person handles being wrong shows their strength. How a person handles being right shows their maturity.

CHAPTER ONE

Age forces you to face the fact that you
have been wrong once or twice and it
could happen again.

The easiest and the most deceitful way to tell
a lie is to first wrap the lie in sacred words.

Sometimes it's not the weight of the world that
you feel on your shoulders but the hands of Heaven
trying to get you to sit down and rest awhile.

Laughter restores what seriousness has stolen.
Your words speak – your intent shouts.

CHAPTER ONE

You do not need to understand the roadblock to use the detour. This life is too short to stop every time you don't understand it.

On your calendar, rename one day of each month Someday. On that day try to work on a few of the things you said you would get to someday.

It is laughable that we live like a child in a car seat holding on tightly to a small plastic steering wheel and seriously believing that we are directing the car.

We spend so much time analyzing and figuring out what is happening that when we decide that it is good, it's gone.

CHAPTER ONE

In each day there are many windows and one
or two doors. The windows are for dreaming and the
doors are for going out to meet your dream.

There are special doors in life that can only
be opened by the person who cries, "Enough!".

You can either complain or make
changes. Doing both at the same time hinders
the rate of change.

Who you are changes with every second's input and
thoughts. So don't ever think that you can figure out
who you are and be done with it.

CHAPTER ONE

There is no such thing as failure as we have been taught. It is merely a misunderstood word used to describe the place where we changed our course.

Do not linger too long in the crossroads. Better to choose wrongly and have the strength to turn around than to not choose and be drained by indecision.

The longer that you wear your mask, the easier it becomes to forget you have it on.

Your ego will sacrifice the peace and tranquility of your body and mind for a moment of being right. It is too heavy a price to pay.

CHAPTER ONE

Cultivate optimism. It multiplies the pleasure of the
good things that happen and lessens the sting
of the bad things.

Support is only available
to those who will not rely on it.

Humility is only a virtue if you have confidence;
otherwise, it's merely surrender.

Don't sit in the basement, ignoring the stairs,
and complain about the view.

A laugh in a home is more nourishing than
a sweet in a temple.

CHAPTER ONE

Does what you want out of life agree perfectly with
what you think about throughout your day?

A fear is the only thing
that can give birth to an excuse.

If you want to know who you really are, watch
your thoughts. The real you is not the thinker
but the watcher.

When you get a grain of sand in your eye you
look for an eye specialist and not a sand
specialist. Deal with what is hurting in you and
not with what hurt you.

A kindness done today is a seed that may
not flower in your lifetime, but a kindness that
is not done today will never flower.

Compassion comes from seeing others actually living
what you have only feared would happen.

Efficiency is a wonderful ability; but without
the addition of wisdom, you will never understand
which things are worth doing slowly.

Nothing is sadder than taking a little game like
"what is wrong with this picture" and making it an
outlook on life.

CHAPTER ONE

Being right merely allows us to continue on our
merry way, but being wrong opens us up to review
and introspection while washing our emotions
and resetting our pomposity.

It is not success or failure that defines who you are.
It is who you credit or blame that defines you.

Forget searching for the meaning of life.
Search for what makes you happy and life has meaning.

There will only be one day on which you will die.
There will be thousands on which you will live.
Your choice: to fear the one or to enjoy the many.

CHAPTER ONE

Fools curse the winds that blow them off balance.
The wise adjust their footing.

You don't have to stop in order to change the
direction of your life. Life, like airplanes, has a
tendency to stall when slowed down too much.

You cannot poison one end of the pool and swim
safely in the other end for very long.

To a loser, failure is the end of the road.
To a winner, failure is the end of a chapter.

If salmon didn't go against the flow at least once,
there wouldn't be any more salmon.

You do not choose every seed that blows into
your garden but you definitely choose which
ones you nurture.

How few of us see the irony of complaining about
our life while sitting on a chair with clean clothes
and a washed body eating a hot meal.

If you are sensitive, you will know that everything
around you affects you. If you are enlightened,
you will know that you affect everything around you.

The past is only true in the past. When
we bring it forward to the present to
discuss it, it is always altered by the journey.

CHAPTER ONE

Never keep the company of anyone to whom
the display of wealth is the basis for their identity.

Uncontrolled spending stems from a confusion
that having more is the same as being more.

WORRY

We find it so hard to live with our problems until
we have a major crisis and then we easily dismiss what
we thought were problems.

Everyone has found a deeper strength in themselves
and learned valuable lessons from a crisis and yet we all
pray that they not befall us.

CHAPTER TWO

The kite that faces the wind flies the highest.

The most important lessons are sometimes
gift wrapped inside the worst days.

It may seem like life is hammering on us at
times but we must remember that we are merely
a chisel and life is creating a masterpiece.

Worries are like mushrooms. They grow the biggest
if left alone in darkness.

Worry is the incredible ability to experience
bad things that never happen.

CHAPTER TWO

In order to successfully worry and complain,
you must first make yourself blind to the love
and blessings in your life.

By its very nature, worrying cannot influence
anything in a positive way.

Sometimes we are like the starving
man who walks through the orchard
of ripe fruit but stays hungry because
he is always looking down.

Worry doesn't prepare you for
tomorrow. It robs you of today.

CHAPTER TWO

A negative thought is light as air and easily
drifts through our consciousness unless we
personalize it and tether it to us with worry.

We can do very little to stop the arrival
of a worrisome thought, but once it has made
an appearance we have two choices:
We can talk ourselves into it or out of it.

Of all of life's pastimes, none
is less productive or more widely
practiced than complaining.

Your reactions tell more about you than
your actions do.

CHAPTER TWO

The basis for most of the worries in
our life is the erroneous belief that this time
it really is serious.

A problem is the name we give to something
that we refuse to accept as it is.

A balanced and centered life is not
a life devoid of things to worry about.
It's just a life devoid of worrying.

Never underestimate the positive power
of a dark period. It is only in total darkness
that the seed sprouts and starts to become
a beautiful flower.

CHAPTER TWO

If you were introduced to an exact copy
of you, what advice would you give?

Yesterday's burdens and worries are
easily dismissed when faced with the
true burdens and worries of today until
we dismiss them tomorrow.

The most futile time is the time we spend
trying to solve the problems of the world as a diversion
to discussing the problems in our hearts.

If you have faith, you can get through most things
without getting too upset. If you have faith
and humor, you can get through anything.

CHAPTER TWO

Oh, the suffering we accept when we choose to live
as a victim because we falsely believe that what
happens to us is more interesting than just being us.

If you think a problem of yours is unsolvable, make
believe it belongs to someone else. We can always come
up with solutions for other peoples' problems.

Most problems just appear and can be solved just
as quickly. It is the useless searching for the problem's
origins instead of solutions that make it complex.

If we don't learn to laugh at our little
missteps in life, we will have great difficulty
recovering from the falls.

CHAPTER TWO

Every crisis is a test to find out if you really believe
all of the advice you have been giving.

Your ability to accept the changes in your life
is in direct proportion to how easily you can laugh.

To change anything, first change your attitude.
The most beautiful moment in life is
that moment when joy fills your heart
because someone else is happy.

All of the yesterdays that you were
sure you would never get through
stand as a stark reminder that this one
is not as difficult as you think.

CHAPTER TWO

Adversity always appears smaller in the rear view
mirror. Maturity comes with the knowledge
that the mountain in front of us will soon be
the molehill behind us.

Kind words and a sense of humor are
the first victims of a negative outlook. Without
them, every day is weakened enough to be
afflicted by worries.

So many good days are wasted watching
for signs that our good days are over.

A large, dangerous illness can knock us
down fast but an insignificant illness and lots
of worry can do it faster.

CHAPTER TWO

The worries that should upset us could fill
a small glass. The worries that we let upset us
could fill a small stadium.

To worry is to ignore Heaven.

Where is there room for happiness if you spend
all of your sunny days preparing for a rainy day?

If you fill your heart with regrets of
yesterday and the worries of tomorrow,
you'll have no room for today's love.

Do not fret about what isn't working in your life; that will
never solve anything. Consider what does work in your
life, no matter its size, and build on that.

As you would bale the water from a boat to travel
well, so, too, must you bale the negativity from
your life in order to live well.

Bring to mind all of your burdens and write them
down. You will soon see that the shadow of the burden
is much larger than its description.

All complaining is an attempt at trying to
convince yourself and others that you are too weak
to change or adapt to the situation.

Everything will not work out the way you
want it to every single time because you are learning,
adjusting and planning and not just planning.

CHAPTER TWO

Problems are the label that we give to the things
in our life that we resist.

The beauty that was there before the storm is still
there during the storm. The only difference is that
we tend to narrow our vision during a storm.

Even though we say we wish to be rid of it, we
often hold onto a problem so that we can explain
to others what we are going through.

A crisis is a precious gift in an ugly package.
It is wrapped that way so that we may easily cast
aside the package and keep only the gift.

CHAPTER TWO

A crisis or problem is not an interruption
of our life's path. It is just a step
that is different from the last one.

Problems in life are like the wind to
a sailboat. Too much wind and it's destroyed.
Too little and it doesn't progress at all.

Worrying is a negative way to be
connected to something or someone.

A thousand paths we could travel, and yet,
we stay on the one that has brought forth so
many of our complaints.

CHAPTER TWO

Understand that our problems definitely
influence part of our life but it is we who give them
permission to affect all of our life.

Never underestimate the negative effect that an
empty stomach can have on a full mind.

We could handle the vast majority of our
discomforts easily if we didn't entertain the
notion that they may get worse.

When you look back on your life you will always
notice that the things that you worried about were not
the things to worry about.

CHAPTER TWO

Worry depends on amnesia for its existence.
We must forget we have overcome many difficulties.

Most people don't have the strength to attempt
something big because they have spent their energy
worrying about things so small.

We can handle any problem in life as long as we
only deal with the problem and not all the drama that
surrounds it. Problems can be solved, drama can't.

Ninety percent of everything you worry about
will never happen and the other ten percent you have
no control over. Let go.

CHAPTER TWO

Take all of your worries, one by one, and
laugh at them. The one or two that remain,
you can deal with.

Don't close your eyes and accuse
the world of being dark.

The most addictive and least productive act
of the mind is in imagining that the past turned out
differently than it really did.

If you keep busy with enough material things,
what's really important will go and sit on your
deathbed and wait for you.

HOPE

Hope is a window that lets you see outside the room
that you are in right now.

We wait so long for conditions to be right to make
a move, unaware that going ahead and making the move
creates the right conditions.

CHAPTER THREE

Sometimes what we perceive as darkness
in our lives is actually the wings of angels
covering us to keep us from harm.

Take a chance. Leave doubt and the
past behind and set sail for your dreams.
An island never came to a ship.

Every single flower and plant that you see,
at some time, disregarded the weight and
the darkness upon them and kept going until
they broke through.

When we have those moments where we feel
like everything is wonderful in our life, we forget
that it was change that took us there.

CHAPTER THREE

It is the blessing of laughter and love on
the other side of sadness that call to lead us
out of the darkness.

You can only start from where you are and you can
only begin in the present. You are obviously in
the right place and time to make anything happen.

You must always make room for hope in your life.
It is the main doorway that all joy comes through.

Love is the voice that assures you that
everything will be all right.

Going through life with optimism is like skiing
down a beautiful hill covered in soft snow. Going
through life with negativity is like skiing down that
same beautiful hill with no snow.

Hope is the gift of a special sight that allows us to see
what is in front of us in the darkness.

The trees, knowing it is time, let go of the leaves they
have held onto so strongly content to possess nothing
but the promise of spring.

Don't be afraid of trying something else even if it
seems fraught with failure. Otherwise we would never
have learned to walk.

CHAPTER THREE

It is love that propels us through life but it is
hope that stands us upright for the journey.

Love is the path we walk. Faith is the gentle
hand pushing on our back. Hope is the vision that
enables us to see where we are going.

Sometimes you must fight, not the debilitating
fight of those who are angry or upset but the
fight of those who know they can change
the direction of their life.

Doing anything worthwhile in life without
focusing your energy is like trying to do successful
laser surgery with a flashlight.

Hope is the always available bridge
that spans the distance between good days.

Crying at midnight because there is no sunrise at the
moment is just as silly as complaining in the middle of
our life that our dreams have not been fulfilled.

HAPPINESS

When you come to a fork in the road of life, always
take the one that glows with passion.

A flower that blooms where no one can see it blooms
with the same intensity as one in the local park.
You don't need to be somewhere else in order to bloom.

CHAPTER FOUR

It's not that anything fundamentally changes when you are happy, it's that you tend to take lightly the things that would normally irritate you.

A change of attitude is only a smile away.

A kind word now is worth more than all the intentions of doing something good when extra money comes in.

Happiness is always your companion. However, you may not be on speaking terms if you have ignored it for too long.

Your dreams for happiness await your action. It is your love that gives them wings. The biggest impediment to our happiness is that when we don't know what to do, we find fault with ourselves.

The key to harmony is making yourself a priority and not making anyone else less than that.

You can be happy all the time if you don't talk yourself out of it.

Learn to just enjoy the moments of bliss. Many times we don't enjoy them because we are too busy wishing for more.

CHAPTER FOUR

What material thing could be as priceless as
peace of mind? So why are "things" still at the top
of your wish list?

If there were one golden key to happiness it
would open the door to the future and lock the
door to the past.

The keys to serenity are to accept where you are,
dream of where you wish to be, and firmly believe that
all that happens is a blessing from Heaven.

The greatest joy is always in giving.
So why do we think that getting a certain
something will make us the happiest?

CHAPTER FOUR

There are two steps to happiness. The first step is
to be aware of the beauty and love in your life at this
moment. Step two is to repeat step one.

Forgiving ourselves is the blessing that
gives us the chance to check our baggage instead
of carrying it.

If we could put aside all of the past hurts that
we righteously cling to for just a moment, we would be
overwhelmed by the love we have been missing.

Everyone agrees that if you act sick long enough,
it will come true. Why then can't we agree that if we
act happy long enough, it, too, will come to pass.

The ability to do something just for fun is
only available to those who are not buried under
a suffocating cloak of what is planned.

Don't ever let your wants make your haves
seem insignificant.

Laughter restores what seriousness has stolen.

The key to happiness is an active, conscious,
once-a-day celebration of what you have
and who you love.

CHAPTER FOUR

We are the ones who construct our checklist for happiness. If everything on that checklist is huge, there is little chance for a happy life.

If you put a few slices of bread in a box and put the box in the middle of a sumptuous buffet and every time you were hungry you went only to that box, you would be living an ordinary life.

So much happiness is never enjoyed because the owner abandons it to go looking for more.

There is peace to be found in each and every moment. It is only our thinking of the past or the future that denies it to us.

CHAPTER FOUR

One of the golden keys to happiness is the
ability to remember the feeling of Sunday afternoon
and realize that that is who you really are.

Happiness is the product of stopping often
enough to enjoy what you have before you continue
the quest for more.

Learn to generate self-compliments as easily
as you generate self-criticism.

One of the golden rules of happiness
is to never allow your net worth to influence
your self-worth.

CHAPTER FOUR

One of the greatest lessons of life that you
must learn is that sometimes you will have to work
at becoming happy.

Attitude, thoughts, actions. Change any one
of the three and the other two will follow.

You must learn how to generate happiness
because you will eventually run out of
places to find it.

There is nothing stopping you from
being happy right now except what you
are thinking about right now.

In order to move faster up the ladder of success
most people lighten their load by tossing
away their humility, compassion, and honesty
and then complain about how empty success
is when they reach the top.

Feeling loved and sharing it with a loved one is
the sign of a lover. Feeling loved and sharing it with
everyone is the sign of a teacher.

Inner peace is not guaranteed to people who relinquish
all that they own but it is guaranteed to the ones
who relinquish the attachment to all that they own.

The first step to freedom is to go inside and take the
whip out of the hands of your memories.

CHAPTER FOUR

It is not enough to just think positively. One
must charge those thoughts with enthusiasm if they
are going to have any chance of surviving.

Never say that you just want to do nothing.
It is completely unobtainable. You are always going
to be doing something. Instead, choose what
you want to be doing.

Going into the past to find an answer is often
futile because we have rewritten the past so often in
our minds that the original no longer exists.

Always have at least one adventure planned in
your thoughts. It is not so much an escape as it is
a reminder of your freedom.

CHAPTER FOUR

The world is a giant, delicious playground to the person
who overcomes the fear of change.

The kindness of a person can easily be
measured by how much they desire to see
someone else succeed.

We dream of the day that we have nothing to do and
yet we forget that real happiness is always about doing
something we love to do.

THE PRESENT

Being in the right place at the right time means very little if your awareness is focused on reliving yesterday.

No matter how hard you try, you can't catch a ball that was missed in the fourth inning in the fifth. But you can miss again in the fifth by focusing on the fourth.

CHAPTER FIVE

We would not wear the clothes of winter in the
season of the sun, so why do we think it is appropriate
to wear yesterday's troubles today?

You have the ability, right now, to bring more peace
into your life than you have ever found on any vacation.
Let go, right now, and choose peacefulness.

The present moment is rarely unbearable in and of
itself. We must burden it with many dark thoughts
of an imagined future in order for it to weigh us down.

Someday your wish may be to reach back through
time and have this moment and these people
to cherish again. What is possible to do now will
be no more than a wish later.

A good day can't be held and kept. Like an ice cream cone in the summer, it has to be enjoyed with pleasure and without pause.

Happiness comes easily to the person who does not try to live yesterday again today.

There is no such thing, in a life so short as ours, as just another day.

The road of life is paved as you live it. Now is your only opportunity to walk barefoot in the sand.

The only thing that you positively can't do on any other day for the rest of your life is enjoy today.

CHAPTER FIVE

In the end, all of your possessions will go to others
with sadness. Give away as much as you can now
so that you may pass these things on with happiness.

If you go forward, it's progression. If you
go backwards, it's regression. If you stay in
the present, it's celebration.

Step confidently into each new day. The day
will not judge you until it is over.

Every day you have the choice to hit the repeat
button and do it all again or to embrace these five
words: every morning, a new beginning.

CHAPTER FIVE

To discover who you are, it is foolish to look at
who you have been. A butterfly would not fly better by
studying a caterpillar.

The farmer who starves to death in an orchard of ripe
fruit because he was too busy planting more trees
is no different from the person who works away each
day planning to enjoy it all someday.

Today is a piece of clay that will harden forever at
midnight as a work of art or a piece of clay.

This day is priceless. If you owned all the treasures
of the world, you could not buy even a second of it
after midnight tonight.

CHAPTER FIVE

TAOWI – Total Acceptance Of What Is. It doesn't
mean that you like what is happening but you refuse
to make believe that it's not happening,

Our greatest chance of success in any area of
our life is always in those things that have our
undivided attention.

This moment is the most fortunate of all because
it is only in this moment that you can truly begin to
change your life.

If the future looks scary and bleak, do not
spend much time there.

CHAPTER FIVE

We find it so easy to understand that we
outgrew the clothes of childhood, but we rarely
consider that we may have outgrown some
of the rules of childhood.

Life goes forward, but we spend so much of our time
looking in the rear view mirror at our past and
then wonder why we didn't see what was coming.

Every time you turn to the past you turn your
back on the future.

Even the most careful trip into the past will stir
up enough dust to affect what we see.

LOVE

To tear apart the rose in search of its beauty is the same
as analyzing a relationship to find the love.

It is in trying to figure out why we love someone
or why they love us that we lose the bliss of
just loving them.

CHAPTER SIX

The road to paradise is paved with the
repetition of the words I love you.

If you look for the love inside of you, it will
hide from you. If you show love to someone else,
it will be apparent to both of you.

Spend your time on how you look,
if you wish, but you will be remembered
most for how you love.

This day is the last day of your life or the first
day of the rest of your life. Either way, there stands the
perfect reason to love the ones you love.

CHAPTER SIX

You'll know when you are filled with love.
There will be no music playing and yet you'll
still want to dance.

We are all looking for something. We don't know exactly
what it is but we do know that when we love, the
search doesn't seem to matter.

If you are fighting for something, fight until
you are defeated. If you are fighting for someone,
never stop fighting.

Look at a clock and it never misses a moment.
Look into the eyes of love and time disappears entirely.

CHAPTER SIX

The poetry and music of this world can only be
truly felt by those who have loved.

Regardless of time or circumstances, love gives
us the powerful ability to alter any thought or any
action to one of beauty.

To know that you have love in your heart is a blessing.
To express that love is the meaning of life.

The most beautiful music in the universe is the sound
of laughter from someone you love.

Many things can make the eyes smile but only
love can make them sparkle.

CHAPTER SIX

A simple test: If you hug someone and never
want to let go, it's love.

Kindness has no expiration date. The kindness that was
done for you in the past can still be passed on.

When you think of someone you love and
a smile crosses your lips, it is a sign that they
just thought of you, too.

Regardless of the weather outside, if you love,
you can close your eyes and see the sunshine.

You don't have to wait until the end of life
to experience Heaven. It's in the next hug with
someone you love.

CHAPTER SIX

When you love, you honor everyone
that ever loved you.

Love is the gentle nudging at the crossroads of
criticism and compassion.

Those who focus on love are shown life's blessings.
Those who focus on things are shown life's drama.

To do anything for someone else in the name
of love is to gild a moment of life.

Life is alternating layers of sour and sweet.
It is only a passionate love that can stir it into
a potion that is always palatable.

CHAPTER SIX

Every heart is covered with the seeds of love.
It is the footprints of others that press the
seeds deeply enough so that they may
begin to grow.

The people who you like will teach you love.
The people who you don't like will teach you love.

Never ignore the little signs of love in order to
find a greater love. For all great love is grown from
little acts of love.

If you consciously fill yourself with love, where
is there room for the things that you thought were
bothering you?

There are kisses and then there are KISSES.
There are hugs and then there are HUGS.
There is love and then there is LOVE.
Try to always live and love in capital letters.

Only love can repair what a lack of love has hurt.

There is a place inside of you that you
can pour in gold and jewels and money
and it never will fill. But if you pour in a little
love, it will fill right up.

Love is not blind. Love gives a vision
so clear that it allows a person to see a hidden
need in another.

CHAPTER SIX

If all of the love in the world were placed
on the wing of a butterfly, it would still fly easily.
Some things may weigh us down but love can
never be a burden.

A loving word to a worried mind is a cool
hand to a fevered brow.

If you have two pianos in a room, whatever
chord you strike on one will cause the other to
vibrate the same chord. To feel love, send love.

Your home should be the center and
not the boundary of your love.

CHAPTER SIX

The tiredness of the body is replenished
by sleep. The tiredness of the soul can
only be replenished by loving.

The days that you live are gold.
The days that you love are diamonds.

There are two times when life feels perfect,
when you are doing something you love
and when you are with someone you love.

Love is like a warm towel out of the dryer
on a cold day.

Love is the only thing in the whole world that will
sustain you if you lose everything else.

CHAPTER SIX

When we are consumed with love, we do not
want to change a thing about living or thinking.
Only love can show us the perfection of life.

There are none who stumble past the doorways
of true love faster than those who have been
blinded by success.

No matter how dark the path might seem, love
will always light a candle and hope will always
keep it burning.

What someone will do for love can last forever,
but what someone will do out of fear will last only
until they overcome the fear.

CHAPTER SIX

If you love someone for a reason, that reason has
a life expectancy. If you love someone and can't explain
why, that love is eternal.

Love that is withheld soon spoils and poisons
the owner.

One of the most important lessons to learn in life
is that when we lose the object of our love, we do not
lose the ability to love.

Temporary happiness can be a product of acquisition,
but lasting happiness can only be a product of love.

Love beckons to all. To some the call is to couple and to
others the call is to fall in love with all of life.

Your happiness is not created by someone you love.
It is created by you loving someone.

Love is like reinforcing rods for concrete.
It helps whatever you build to be nearly indestructible.

If you can rationally explain why you love someone,
it's friendship. If the feeling that you have for someone is
beyond words, it's love.

To know that you are loved is to comprehend that
everything else in your life is only a side dish.

If you forgive and don't forget, the person that you
forgave is free but you are still a prisoner.

CHAPTER SIX

If there are enough dotted lines, we can easily
describe the picture. If there are enough moments
of love, we can easily describe the life.

You can't always make someone you love
healthier, but it is usually within your power
to make them happier.

Fear and pain respond well to oil of love.
Oil of love is made by taking love and
mixing it with awareness and compassion
and distilling away the self.

Love, not words, is the only key that can open
a heart that has been locked from the inside.

CHAPTER SIX

Love that is rarely in the thoughts
will soon disappear from the heart.

If we centered all of our love and affection and
attention on every single child born from this
moment on, we would have the world we dream
about in one generation.

You don't help other people by showing how
fat you got at the banquet of life. You help them
by holding their hand and bringing them to
the banquet.

HEALTH

If a gardener spent all of his time commenting
on other gardens, he would starve. Tend to your
own garden first.

The gift of sickness is the forced retreat into
quietness to heal. It is in the quietness that we can
hear the angel of balance whispering to us.

CHAPTER SEVEN

We overwork ourselves to the point of sickness
so that we can finally take time off, without
too much guilt, to hopefully heal the damage
we have done.

If you wish to accomplish more, you
must relax more. Additional tension does not
bring additional success.

If we focused more on the quality of our life,
we would automatically focus less on the
length of our life.

First, fall in love with life. Second, look for someone
who is full of life. Third, mix well and enjoy.

CHAPTER SEVEN

The person who uses guilt is no better than
the person who uses poison. For good health,
avoid them both.

Don't try to change the thing that upsets you. Better
to change the part of you that gets upset.

The easiest way to release yourself from being in
a rut is to go and take a class in something that you
would never have considered.

Feel the way you want to feel regardless of what's
going on around you, and you'll do well regardless
of what's going on around you.

CHAPTER SEVEN

You can have much of everything, but if you have too
little sleep and silence, it will never be enjoyed.

Tiredness is the harbinger of wonderful beginnings.
It is only when we are truly tired of something
that we search and eventually find the strength
to change it.

An awareness of being depressed gives us the
opportunity to do something about it, but most
times we would rather re-label ourselves as serious
and do nothing about it.

The most obvious warning sign of imbalance in our
health or well-being is an unwillingness to help others.

CHAPTER SEVEN

An empty stomach is a poor pedestal for reason.

Never underestimate the ability of stress to cloud your vision.

Every meal regardless of size, requires a smile and a blessing for it to be helpful to the body.

Too often we beggingly search for strength when a good dose of merriment would do us more good.

Irritation is a signal to look inside for imbalance and not a signal to look outside for a target.

One of the biggest mistakes in evaluating our
physical well-being is the misinterpretation of
having so much energy when actually we have
so much tension.

We are given far more good days than bad days.
The key to joyfulness is to allow all the good days
to affect the bad and not the reverse.

STRENGTH

If you believe that it is meant to be, you can get over any hurdle. Never let the hot sand keep you away from the cool waters.

We often give up and blame our lack of progress on not having the most up-to-date tools. The Grand Canyon was carved with water.

CHAPTER EIGHT

Just because a door is closed does not mean
that it is locked. Push against the obstacles in your life,
most will let you through.

There are two times in your life when you need to
be strong and loving: daytime and nighttime.

People who won't forgive are not mean. They are merely
too weak to let it go. Forgiveness takes great strength.

When we get upset, a strong person goes looking
for a solution. A weak person goes looking for blame.

Sometimes it takes more strength to stop climbing
than to continue.

CHAPTER EIGHT

Your emotions are heavily influenced by your
environment. If you don't like the mood you're in,
find the music or the environment that will
help to change it.

By jumping for the star that you couldn't reach,
you unknowingly jump over the gap you wouldn't
dare to breech.

Nobody ever changed their life for the better by
doing it timidly. If you are going to change, make it
a robust, exciting change.

No one ever crossed a chasm in little steps.

CHAPTER EIGHT

There is a champion inside of you. Allow it to set your
posture and guide your thoughts.

Inner strength can be easily measured by the speed
in which a person shifts the blame to another. The faster
the shift, the weaker the strength.

There is a great deal of strength gained by those who
confine a bad morning to the morning.

We all wish for the best of days but it is the worst
of days that straightens our back and brings the fire that
burns away our weaknesses.

CHAPTER EIGHT

In order for you to have the power to stand up
for yourself, you have to tell yourself
that you are going to feel terribly uncomfortable
and it's okay.

Intimidation by another person can
only succeed if it finds a fear inside of us
to power it. Work on conquering the
fear, not the person.

The great test of our strength is what we do next
when a lie presents itself as the easiest way out.

A great deal of your strength comes from those
times that you were not allowed to give up.

CHAPTER EIGHT

Power comes from learning to prioritize and then
dealing with each thing individually, in that
moment, as if it were the only thing in the world.

Making mistakes does not bring growth.
Making mistakes and taking responsibility
for them does.

ANGER

Full minds and empty stomachs are the birthplace
of the harshest words.

Anger and crankiness feel right if we can
justify them but accepting them as right closes the
door to any growth.

CHAPTER NINE

The easiest way to change your attitude is to smile.
A broad smile, even if forced, sends a signal to your
body and mind that everything is all right.

Irritation is not something to be suppressed.
It is something to be acknowledged for it is always
the harbinger of change.

Frustration is a sign and not a penalty. Frustration
arises, like a warning siren, when we believe that we
are in charge of all of the changes in our life.

In our wisdom, we laugh at the pouting child
who refuses to see all the happiness around
him and then we go home and refuse to talk to
anyone because we're mad.

CHAPTER NINE

Your strength comes from living your life. Your agitation
comes from wanting to influence another's.

A momentary pause and a deep breath may not
seem powerful, but they are strong enough to stop the
full force of a hurtful response.

Anger is an unproductive response to the inevitable
intrusion of unhappiness.

Anger makes a person blind to the blessings in life,
but more importantly, it also makes a person deaf
to the whispers of Heaven.

The space between an angry thought and an angry
word is full of opportunity.

CHAPTER NINE

Helpfulness is the natural outpouring of a loving heart.
Criticism is the offspring of anger and pride dressed
up to look like helpfulness.

It is not the simple irritations that bring on a dark
mood. It is our penchant for wrapping a simple
irritation with past events that makes it formidable.

Many kinds of walls are built to hide a tender
heart but none is more impenetrable than the one that
is fortified with sarcasm.

Those who would blame fate because there are no
flowers in their garden would do well to check and see
what seeds they're planting.

CHAPTER NINE

There is no blessing gained by holding your
tongue if you allow every other part of you to
scream out its opinion.

Anger is like a sudden splash of mud
on your windshield. Your ability to perceive
things clearly is directly related to how
fast you can get rid of it.

Anger is a reaction. Staying angry is a choice.

Getting angry at someone who is angry
in order to change that person's
attitude is like trying to put out a fire
with a highway flare.

CHAPTER NINE

The alchemist's dream of turning lead into
gold is minuscule compared with the ability to turn
anger into compassion.

Revenge is like holding the sharp blade of a knife
and beating someone with the handle. We are bound
to hurt ourselves more.

Do not curse the mountain for being in the way.
It amuses the mountain but does nothing for your peace
of mind. Simply go around it.

No one would willingly let the devastation of anger
inside of themselves. That is why anger always gains
admission disguised as the sweetness of righteousness.

CHAPTER NINE

Annoyances are the road flares that tell us that if we
continue on this path, there is a wreck up ahead.

CHAPTER TEN

RELATIONSHIPS

When you do something to spite someone else,
at that moment you are making their displeasure more
important than your happiness. You lose.

Everyone in your life has a gift for you. Some are
in an out stretched hand but the most important
ones are hidden.

CHAPTER TEN

If someone you love irritates you, you still have the
love. But if you refuse to communicate honestly about the
irritation, you are in danger of losing the love.

Some people are with us to teach us love
and some people will leave us to teach us strength.

It is the trees that refuse to bend that groan the loudest.

There is but one force that you must control in
your life and that is the uncontrollable urge to be right.
Unchecked, nothing is more devastating.

Sometimes, what you say can show your intelligence
and sometimes, what you don't say can show your love.

CHAPTER TEN

We want food, we go get it.
We want clothes, we go get them.
We want a movie, we go get it.
We want friendship, we sit and wait.
Why?

That you are alive is self evident: that you have ever
lived is evident to anyone you've ever helped.

You can get closer to the sky by standing on
someone's shoulders but you can only get closer to
Heaven by holding their hand.

If you offer three compliments for every complaint,
you will have success and friends for life.

CHAPTER TEN

It's sad and difficult to be away from the one you love, but it teaches us to focus on their love and to hold them dearly in our thoughts. The key to happiness is to do that when you are with them.

Comparing a person's problems to someone with greater problems never helps.

The greatest barometer of a person's capacity for kindness is most evident in how they treat others when they themselves feel bad.

People will usually love you the way that you love yourself. Your treatment of you is usually the only example for them to follow.

CHAPTER TEN

Our condemnation of anyone else
stems simply from the fact that they don't do
something like we would.

Showing someone that you love them, no matter
how dearly or often, will never take the place of telling
someone that you love them.

There is no winter's cold that penetrates as deeply
as the cold of a heart that will not forgive.

If we were granted the revenge we seek
when we believe we were wronged, we would live
the rest of our life filled with guilt and remorse.
Forgive and prosper.

CHAPTER TEN

If we can force ourselves to think of just one good
attribute of someone we dislike, we would begin to
regain the power that our conditioning took away.

One of the most crippling things to any relationship,
business or personal, is the absurd reliance on hinting.
Cast aside fear and say what you want to say.

If you treat a relationship as if you are the only
one in it, eventually you will be.

If you want to be like a magician and make someone
disappear, first you must take them for granted.

Humor has its place but it should never be used as
a package to deliver ill feelings.

CHAPTER TEN

When we talk from the heart, we must take care
not to alter the words because of how we think the
listener will react.

The easiest way to really know a person's character
is to notice whom they consider to be a success.

Expectations that are not communicated will
surely be unfulfilled.

You grow in a strong, positive way when you use words
instead of looks or attitudes to convey your feelings.

The other person in a relationship is always
responding to what we actually show them and not
to who we are in our own minds.

CHAPTER TEN

Hating someone that was formerly in your life
is a sneaky way of staying connected. Only when all
emotion ceases are they truly gone from your life.

Friends are the unseen rocks that make it look
and feel like we are walking on water.

When speaking about a hurt, don't sugar coat
the words. Sweetening the words to overcome the fear
of an unfavorable reaction is cowardice.

To put the needs of others before our wants is
the road to liberation. To put the wants of others before
our needs is the road to sorrow and humiliation.

To say that you love someone and then allow them to treat you poorly is to admit you know nothing of love. Respect of self is the birthplace of love.

Some people are in our life just to help us to find the strength that is necessary to leave them.

Words that are spoken are perennial and rise again and again. So when speaking to someone you love, hold fast to any word that you do not wish to see again.

If something that you need to sustain your life is a mile underwater, what use is it? Of what use is love that is covered in anger and unkindness?

CHAPTER TEN

Sometimes the most loving thing you can do is
to let another person go. The new freedom is for their
growth, the new pain is for yours.

If you don't treat yourself with respect, other people
will follow your example.

Humor can pave some of the potholes in the
road of life but too often it is used as a detour to keep
someone away from a heart that needs healing.

Never belittle any one else's problems. It may
be an insignificant sliver of wood to you but to them
it's a painful splinter that needs to be dealt with.

CHAPTER TEN

In our childhood the word "No" was always associated with something bad and so we have learned to say "Yes" to everything we are asked to do and seek a "Yes" from everybody. It's time to discard that one.

CHILDREN

Encourage the young to make mistakes. The mistakes
of youth can ruin a day or week. The same mistakes
as an adult can ruin a year or a life.

If you had a great childhood, share what you
learned with a child. If you had a bad childhood,
share what you learned with a child.

CHAPTER ELEVEN

Your children are not born with your fears,
they catch them like a cold from you.

No morning describes the whole day and no
childhood describes the whole person.

If you tell a child his or her place
in the world, they will believe you
for the rest of their lives.

Tolerance is when you look down on
a child and tell them it's probably
okay. Love is when you hug a child and
you both know it's okay.

CHAPTER ELEVEN

It is a sign of your character how you handle someone
who makes the same mistake that you once made.

Give a child a gift and you increase what
that child has. Praise a child and you increase
who that child is.

You can spend all of the time you possibly
can with your children or you can wait a few years and
spend all of your time with their problems.

You may choose either frustration or laughter when you
realize that the things that you didn't listen to as a child,
you now want to teach to a child.

CHAPTER ELEVEN

Good words will guide a child for days.
A good example will guide them for life.

Trying to help a child by criticizing them
is like throwing them a burning rope to help them
climb out of a hole.

FAITH

Aloneness is an absence of people.
Loneliness is an absence of faith.

We look around at the beauty and complexity
in creation and see Heaven. We look at our
own lives and foolishly see only ourselves as
if we were not part of creation.

CHAPTER TWELVE

It is your beliefs and not your place in life that
determines how many choices are available.

Heaven gives water to some and clay to
others but they would never need each other
if He gave everyone bricks.

Of all the things that could possibly happen to you,
the chances of you preparing for the right
one is minimal. Faith and love are the only
umbrellas that cover them all.

Faith is the ability to believe that no matter what
befalls us, there will never be a time when there is not
an outstretched hand in front of us.

CHAPTER TWELVE

If you were to behold a great treasure off
in the distance, what would it matter if the road
to it were bumpy?

Serenity comes from being open to change.
Growth in life is often preceded by an uprooting
of learned assurances.

Knowing how to fit everything into a few hours
can improve your day, but knowing how to do nothing
for a few hours can improve your life.

Never let an answer stop your questing if it
doesn't feel like the right answer. An answer is only
THE answer until a better one shows up.

CHAPTER TWELVE

Eternity doesn't start when you die.
Eternity does not have a beginning.

One doesn't automatically mellow with age.
It is the memory of all the mistakes we made
that allow for the slight possibility of being
wrong once more.

How silly to try to feel connected to the world
by watching or reading the news. That just connects
you to the business of news production.

Knowledge comes from words. Wisdom
comes from silence.

CHAPTER TWELVE

Wisdom gives us the ability to place more importance on the lesson learned then on the suffering associated with it at the time.

A great moment is when you realize that you can have it all. An even greater moment is when you realize that you already have it all.

Laughter is such a blessing that Heaven allows everything else to be blocked out while we enjoy it.

We would never turn away a gift because we did not like the wrapping and yet there are teachers in our life that we ignore because of their appearance.

CHAPTER TWELVE

Getting upset is not a step backwards on the
path of spirituality. Staying upset is.

Turning to Heaven doesn't shorten the journey
by even one step but it does light the way.

Your job is to light the path for others.
When you coerce someone into walking that path,
you will suddenly realize that you have left it.

Effort is up to you. Attainment is up to Heaven.

Heaven often gives us more than we can handle;
otherwise, we would never learn how to surrender
to a higher power.

CHAPTER TWELVE

Trees are the vocal cords of the earth. As the
wind blows through them, they speak to us of things
both peaceful and Divine.

There is no better feeling than when you
send your words to Heaven and something happens
to let you know, beyond the shadow of a doubt,
that you were heard.

Anyone can figure out how many yesterdays they have
had, but only Heaven knows how many tomorrows.

The self test for how much we believe in a Divine
order is to watch our own response to
anyone that we perceive is doing wrong and
apparently getting away with it.

CHAPTER TWELVE

The person who can recite sacred words will receive acclaim, but the person who lives the sacred words will get peace.

If you know, it is enough. If you doubt, you are doomed to buying T-shirts and bumper stickers to advertise that you don't doubt.

Willingness to change and faith are the golden keys that unlock the door to opportunity.

A prayer is a wish with an address on it.

When things look dark, remind yourself that there's always a prayer to hold onto at the end of every rope.

CHAPTER TWELVE

A second sight is given to those who close
their eyes in prayer.

If we could only see the irony of standing on two
fine legs with a voice as strong as steel cursing the
Heavens for forgetting about us.

A disappointment can only be tempered with faith
that a higher power has corrected your course so that
you may miss a bigger storm.

Your path is divinely built, and you can
walk nowhere else. Now, whether you constantly
bounce off the guard rails or walk in peace,
that part is up to you.

CHAPTER TWELVE

It is not by lack of blessings that we feel unfortunate.
It is in the comparison to the perceived blessings of
others that we belittle our own.

Watch a hawk the way he plans and then swoops;
if he misses, he goes to a high place and starts again.

When you hear a beautiful love song, try putting Heaven as
the object of the song and see how wonderful you feel.

We don't criticize a rosebud for not being a flower.
We just wait with a firm and easy faith that it
will be beautiful.

CHAPTER TWELVE

If you wish to elicit the laughter of Heaven,
act like you're alone.

Many people yell to Heaven to accomplish what could
be done with a whisper to themselves.

Anxiety is the feeling that something is going to happen
that you can't handle. Faith is the feeling that something
is always happening and being handled.

Just because you are feeling scared on a roller coaster
doesn't mean that it's out of control.

CHAPTER TWELVE

Those who seek a level of wealth in order to find peace will always be thwarted. Those who seek peace will always be able to handle their level of wealth.

You do not have to own something to appreciate it. That's why Heaven put the stars out of reach but not out of sight.

CPSIA information can be obtained at www.ICGtesting.com
Printed in the USA
LVOW05s1753051213

364050LV00001B/56/P